Thank you for your purchase! If you enjoy this book, please help us with an honest review.

All rights reserved. No part of this book may be reproduced, stored in any retrieval system, or transmitted in any form or by any means, mechanical, photocopying, recording, or otherwise, without the prior permission of the author.

CURSIVE HANDWRITING WORKBOOK ANIMALS

PART 1. Letters

PART 2. Words and sentences

PART 3. Animal riddles

PART 1

Write letters in cursive

PART 1. LETTERS

- Trace the alphabet
- Trace the lowercase and the uppercase letter
- Enjoy it!

Cursive Alphabet

Aa Bb Cc Dd Ee
Ff Gg Hh Ii Jj
Kk Ll Mm Nn
Oo Pp Qq Rr Ss
Tt Uu Vv Ww
Xx Yy Zz

Cursive Alphabet

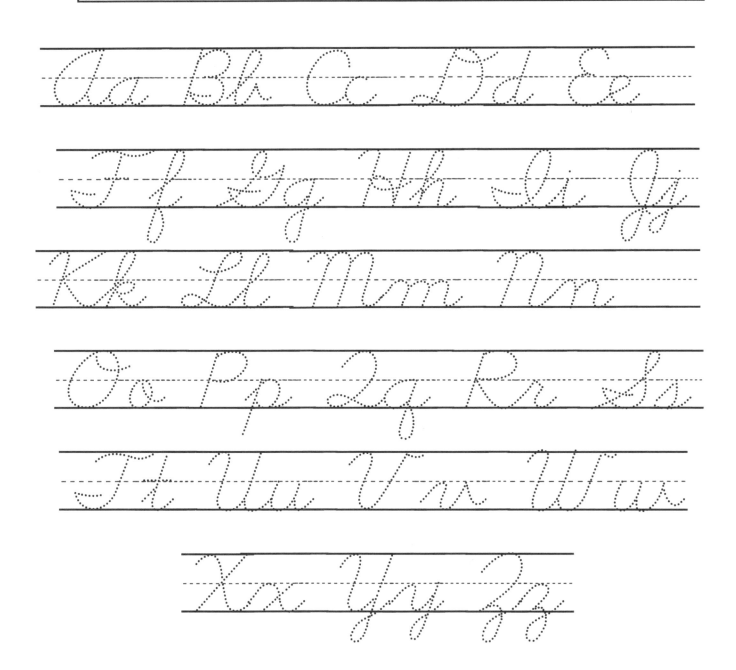

A is for Ant

a *a a a a a a a*
a a a a a a a

a a a a a a a a

A is for Alligator

a *a a a a a a*
a a a a a a a
a a a a a a a

C is for Cat

C is for Cow

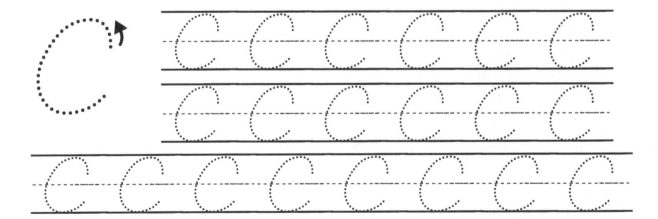

D is for Dinosaur

D is for Duck

E is for Elephant

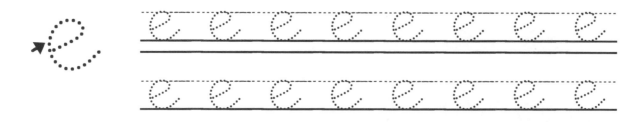

E is for Eagle

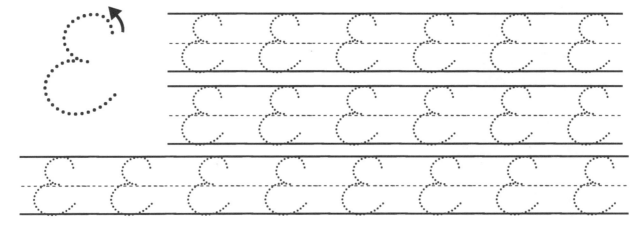

H is for Hamster

H is for Hyena

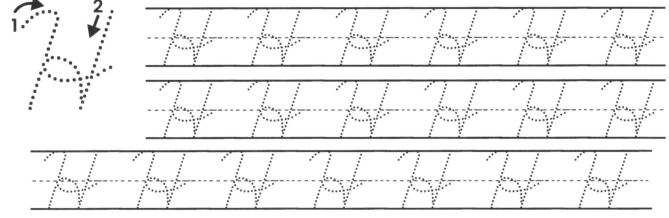

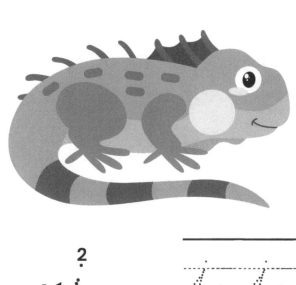

I is for Iguana

I is for Insect

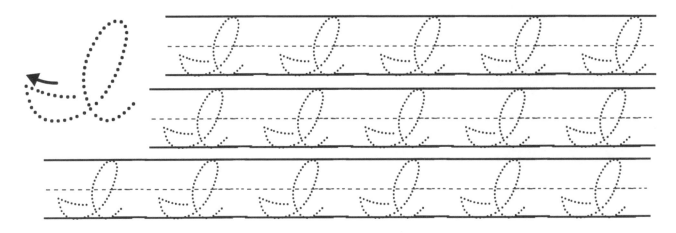

M is for Monkey

M is for Mouse

N is for Narwhal

N is for Nutria

O is for Owl

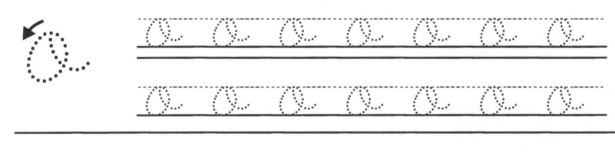

O is for Octopus

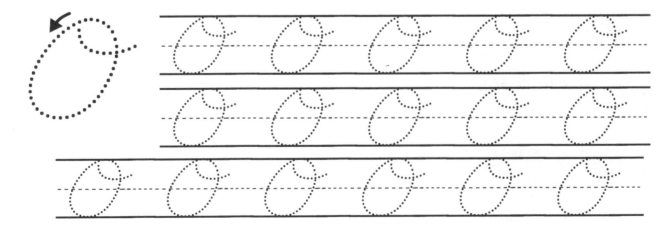

P is for Penguin

P is for Panda

2 is for Quail

R is for Rhinoceros

R is for Raccoon

S is for
Sheep

S is for
Shark

T is for Turtle

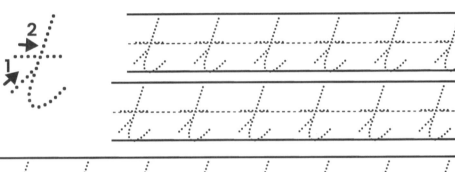

T is for Tucan

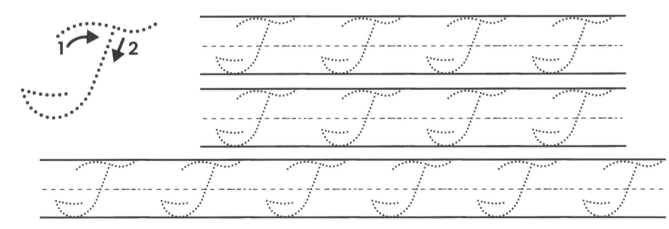

U is for Unicorn

V is for Vampire Bat

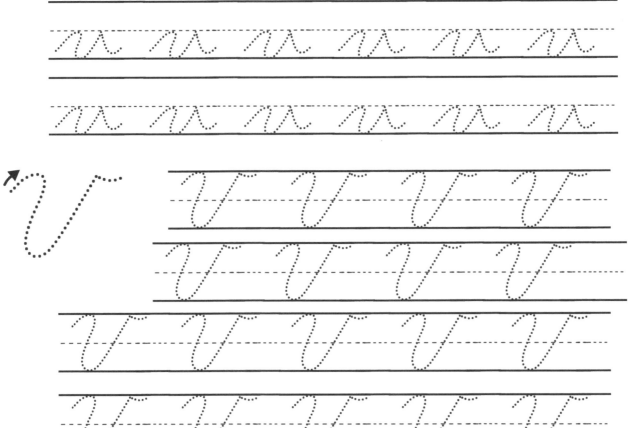

W is for Whale

W is for Wasp

X is for Xerus

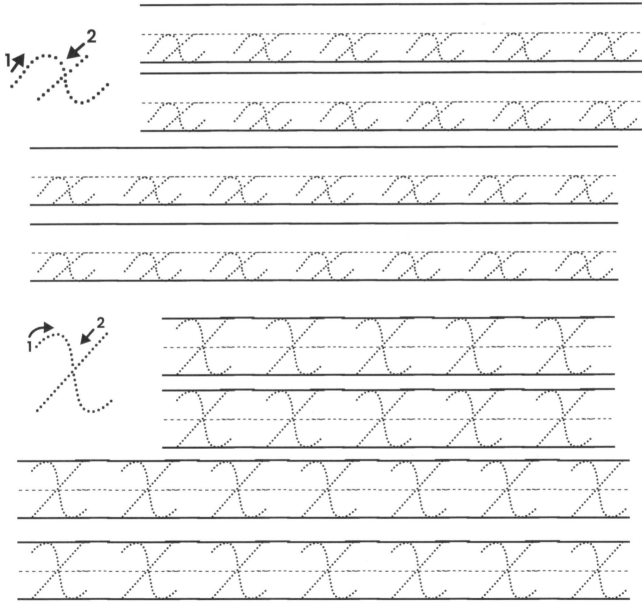

Z is for Zebra

PART 2

Animal words and sentences

4

PART 2. WORDS AND SENTENCES

- Color the animal
- Trace the letters
- Write again the words by yourself
- Trace the sentences
- Write again the sentences by yourself
- Enjoy it!

Aa Aa Aa Aa Aa Aa Aa

Ant Ant Ant Ant Ant

Did you know?

Ants are brown and red insects.

Ants work together as a team to build their homes.

Busy ant, tiny ant and grand

Bb Bb Bb Bb Bb Bb Bb Bb

Bear Bear Bear Bear Bear

Did you know?

Bears are strong swimmers.

Some bears like to take long naps during winter.

Clare the bear, playful and rare.

Cc

Cc Cc Cc Cc Cc Cc Cc Cc Cc

Cat Cat Cat Cat Cat Cat Cat

Did you know?

Cats use their whiskers to explore

Cats purr when they are happy and content

Cute cat, soft and fat

D d

Dd Dd Dd Dd Dd Dd

Duck Duck Duck Duck

Did you know?

Ducks swim in the pond

Ducks waddle when they walk on land

Ducklings quack if they are back

Ee

Ee Ee Ee Ee Ee Ee Ee Ee Ee

Elephant Elephant Elephant

Did you know?

Elephants have long trunks

Big ears help elephants stay cool in hot weather

Elephant dance, big and elegant

F f

F f F f F f F f F f F f F f

Frog Frog Frog Frog Frog

Did you know?

Frogs start as tadpoles in the pond

Amphibians like frogs can live on land and in water

Jumping frog sitting in a log

G g

Gg Gg Gg Gg Gg Gg Gg Gg

Giraffe Giraffe Giraffe Giraffe

Did you know?

Giraffes eat leaves from tall trees.

A group of giraffes is called a tower.

Giraffe's grace in the wild space.

Hh

Hh Hh Hh Hh Hh Hh Hh Hh

Hyena Hyena Hyena Hyena

Did you know?

Hyenas have strong jaws.

A hyena's laughter can be heard for miles.

Hyena's chuckle in the savanna's puzzle.

Ii

Ii Ii Ii Ii Ii Ii Ii Ii

Iguana Iguana Iguana

Did you know?

Baby iguanas are called hatchlings.

Long tails help iguanas balance as they climb.

Iguana on a banana a sunny cabana.

Did you know?

Some jellyfish glow in the dark

Jellyfish don't have a brain or a heart

Jellyfish dance, in a watery trance

K k

Kk Kk Kk Kk Kk Kk Kk Kk

Koala Koala Koala Koala Koala

Did you know?

Koalas sleep a lot in trees

Koalas are known for their calm and cuddly demeanor

Koala in a tree so carefree

Ll

Ll Ll Ll Ll Ll Ll Ll Ll

Lion Lion Lion Lion Lion

Did you know?

Lions are majestic big cats in Africa

Lions are symbols of strength and courage

Majestic lion with a fierce golden scion

Mm

Mm Mm Mm Mm Mm Mm

Monkey Monkey Monkey

Did you know?

Monkeys swing and play in the trees.

Monkeys groom each other to show affection.

Playful monkey is so spunky.

Nn

Nn Nn Nn Nn Nn Nn Nn

Nutria Nutria Nutria Nutria

Did you know?

Nutrias love to live near water

Nutrias eat plants, leaves, and aquatic vegetation

Nutria by the river, a sleek swimmer

Oo

Oo Oo Oo Oo Oo Oo Oo Oo

Owl Owl Owl Owl Owl

Did you know?

Owls live in trees and quite forests

Owls can turn their heads almost 360 degrees

Wise old owl, in the nighttime prowl

Pp

Pp Pp Pp Pp Pp Pp Pp Pp Pp

Panda Panda Panda Panda

Did you know?

Pandas are black and white

Pandas live in bamboo forests in China

Panda in bamboo, a cuddly view

Qq

Qq Qq Qq Qq Qq Qq Qq Qq

Quail Quail Quail Quail

Did you know?

Quails are beautiful social birds.

Male quails often have colorful plumage.

Quail's soft tale, in the evening's dale

Rr

Rr Rr Rr Rr Rr Rr Rr Rr Rr

Rhinoceros Rhinoceros Rhinoceros

Did you know?

Rhinos love to bathe in the mud

Rhinos are herbivores, eating plants and leaves

Rhino on the grass, a massive mass

Ss *Ss* *Ss* *Ss* *Ss* *Ss* *Ss* *Ss*

Sheep *Sheep* *Sheep* *Sheep*

Did you know?

Sheep say baa when they vocalize

Lambs are baby sheep, cute and small

Sheep in a pen, fluffy wool again

Tt

Tt Tt Tt Tt Tt Tt Tt

Turtle Turtle Turtle Turtle

Did you know?

Turtles have a hard shell.

Land turtles are also called tortoises.

Turtle in the sand, slow and grand.

Uu

Uu Uu Uu Uu Uu Uu Uu Uu

Unicorn Unicorn Unicorn

Did you know?

Unicorns are mythical creatures

Unicorns are associated with
fantasy tales

Unicorn so rare, with a magical flair

Vv

Vv Vv Vv Vv Vv Vv

Vampire bat Vampire bat

Did you know?

Vampire bats feed on blood

Vampire bats play a crucial role in ecosystems

Vampire bat, in the moon's quiet chat

Ww

Ww Ww Ww Ww Ww

Whale Whale Whale Whale

Did you know?

Whales are marine mammals

Some whales, like the blue whale, are massive

Whale in the sea, majestic and free

Xx

Xx Xx Xx Xx Xx Xx Xx

Xenia Xenia Xenia Xenia Xenia

Did you know?

Xerus is a type of squirrel.

Xerus is also known as an African ground squirrel.

Xerus on the ground, digging all around.

Yy

Yy Yy Yy Yy Yy Yy Yy

Yak Yak Yak Yak Yak Yak

Did you know?

Yaks have long, curved horns

Yaks are native to the Himalayan region

Yak on the hill, standing still

Zz Zz Zz Zz Zz Zz Zz Zz

Zebra Zebra Zebra Zebra Zebra

Did you know?

Each zebra's stripe pattern is unique

Zebras are herbivores, grazing on grass and plants

Zebra in the grass, stripes that amass

PART 3

Animal Riddles

PART 3. ANIMALS RIDDLES

- Read the question
- Trace the question
- Write it by yourself
- Answer the question with the name of an animal
- Write it by yourself
- Enjoy it!

QUESTION

Who purrs and has fur saying meow?

Who purrs and has fur saying meow?

ANSWER

cat cat cat cat cat cat cat cat cat cat cat

QUESTION

Gentle giants with kind, big eyes

Gentle giants with kind, big eyes

ANSWER

QUESTION

What big grey animal has a big trunk?

ANSWER

QUESTION

What furry friend barks and wags its tail?

What furry friend barks and wags its tail?

ANSWER

D

QUESTION

What pink farm animal says oink-oink?

What pink farm animal says oink-oink?

ANSWER

P

QUESTION

What long reptile has no legs?

What long reptile has no legs?

ANSWER

s

QUESTION

What creature scuttles sideways on the beach?

ANSWER

C

QUESTION

What tiny insect has colorful spots and wings?

ANSWER

L

QUESTION

What farm animal says 'moo' and gives milk?

What farm animal says 'moo' and gives milk?

ANSWER

c

QUESTION

What big and furry animal loves honey?

What big and furry animal loves honey?

ANSWER

B

QUESTION

What green friend hops and loves to croak?

What green friend hops and loves to croak?

ANSWER

F

QUESTION

What cute black and white bear eats bamboo?

ANSWER

Printed in Poland
by Amazon Fulfillment
Poland Sp. z o.o., Wrocław